DISCOVER
THE OCEANS

Pacific Ocean

by Emily Rose Oachs

BELLWETHER MEDIA • MINNEAPOLIS, MN

Note to Librarians, Teachers, and Parents:

Blastoff! Readers are carefully developed by literacy experts and combine standards-based content with developmentally appropriate text.

Level 1 provides the most support through repetition of high-frequency words, light text, predictable sentence patterns, and strong visual support.

Level 2 offers early readers a bit more challenge through varied simple sentences, increased text load, and less repetition of high-frequency words.

Level 3 advances early-fluent readers toward fluency through increased text and concept load, less reliance on visuals, longer sentences, and more literary language.

Level 4 builds reading stamina by providing more text per page, increased use of punctuation, greater variation in sentence patterns, and increasingly challenging vocabulary.

Level 5 encourages children to move from "learning to read" to "reading to learn" by providing even more text, varied writing styles, and less familiar topics.

Whichever book is right for your reader, Blastoff! Readers are the perfect books to build confidence and encourage a love of reading that will last a lifetime!

This edition first published in 2016 by Bellwether Media, Inc.

No part of this publication may be reproduced in whole or in part without written permission of the publisher. For information regarding permission, write to Bellwether Media, Inc., Attention: Permissions Department, 5357 Penn Avenue South, Minneapolis, MN 55419.

Library of Congress Cataloging-in-Publication Data

Oachs, Emily Rose.
    Pacific Ocean / by Emily Rose Oachs.
        pages cm – (Blastoff! Readers: Discover the Oceans)
    Includes bibliographical references and index.
    Summary: "Simple text and full-color photography introduce beginning readers to the Pacific Ocean. Developed by literacy experts for students in kindergarten through third grade"—Provided by publisher.
    Audience: Ages 5-8.
    Audience: K to grade 3.
    ISBN 978-1-62617-333-0 (hardcover : alk. paper)
    1. Pacific Ocean–Juvenile literature. I. Title.
    GC771.O23 2016
    910.9164–dc23

                        2015031571

Printed in the United States of America, North Mankato, MN.

Table of **Contents**

The Largest Ocean   4

Where Is the Pacific Ocean?   6

The Climate and Features   8

Ring of Fire   12

The Plants and Animals   16

Fast Facts About the
   Pacific Ocean   20

Glossary   22

To Learn More   23

Index   24

The Largest Ocean

The Pacific Ocean is the world's largest ocean. It is two times bigger than the Atlantic Ocean, the second largest.

The explorer Ferdinand Magellan named the Pacific Ocean. The ocean's name means "peaceful."

DID YOU KNOW?

- The Mariana Trench is more than 35,000 feet (10,668 meters) below the Pacific Ocean's surface. It is the deepest known point on Earth.

- The Pacific Ocean covers more of Earth than all its dry land combined!

- Kelp may stretch 100 feet (30 meters) from the ocean's floor.

- Some leatherback sea turtles cross the Pacific Ocean to find food. They can swim more than 8,000 miles (12,875 kilometers)!

leatherback sea turtle

Where Is the Pacific Ocean?

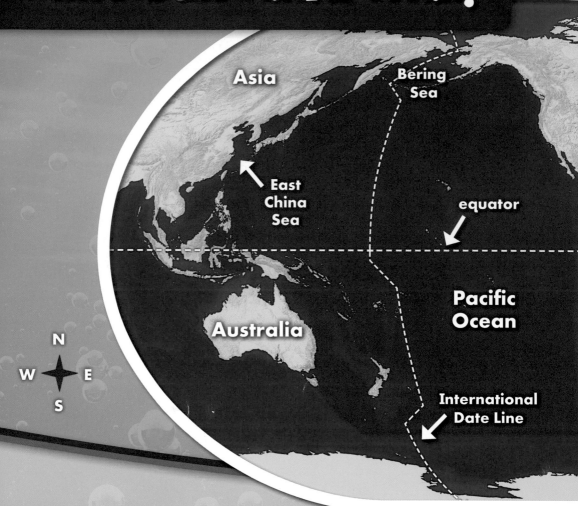

The Pacific Ocean rests in all four **hemispheres**. The **equator** cuts through it. The ocean flows into the East China, Bering, and other seas.

North
America

South
America

Australia lies to the ocean's
southwest. To the northwest is Asia.
North and South America are to
the east.

The Climate and Features

Much of the Pacific Ocean's **climate** is warm and **tropical**. Waters get colder farther north and south of the equator.

Typhoons may form over the Pacific Ocean. These storms bring strong winds and rain. Every few years, **El Niño** happens. It causes weather to change around the world.

typhoon

Ocean **currents** meet near South America's Galápagos Islands. They bring sea life to the islands. Bottlenose dolphins and green sea turtles swim in the waves.

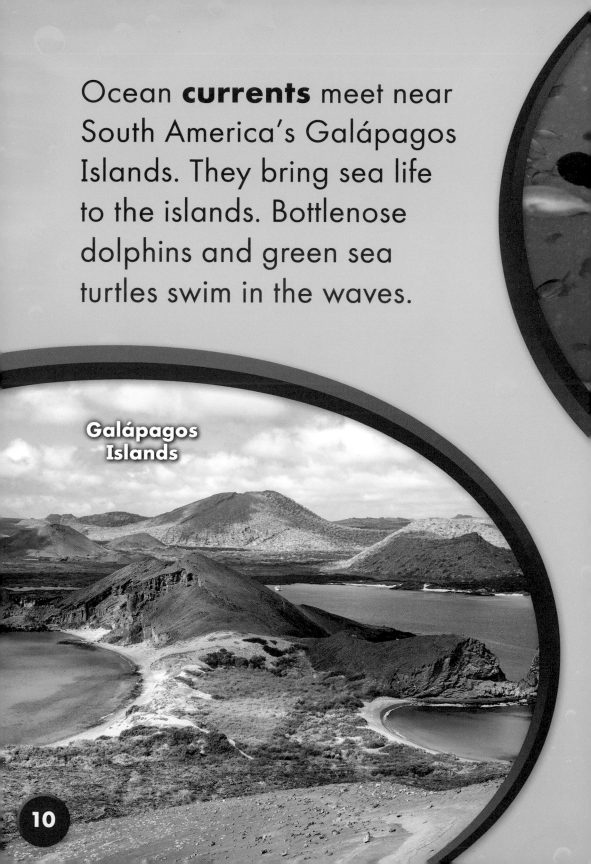

Galápagos Islands

Great
Barrier Reef

The Great Barrier Reef is also home to many colorful creatures. This **coral reef** lies off Australia's northeastern coast.

Ring of Fire

Along the Pacific Ocean's edges is a belt of underwater **volcanoes**. They are part of the Ring of Fire. Its U-shape stretches about 25,000 miles (40,000 kilometers).

More than 450 volcanoes are in the Ring of Fire! Mountains and **trenches** are also there.

N
W E
S

Ring of Fire

Large moving **plates** of rock make up Earth's surface. The Ring of Fire lies where plates meet under the ocean.

Sometimes, a plate moves under another. This creates trenches. **Earthquakes** happen when plates rub together.

The Plants and Animals

kelp

Seagrass grows along the Pacific Ocean's tropical coasts. Near the water's surface, krill eat floating **phytoplankton**.

krill

sea otter

sea urchin

Kelp grows by the ocean's rocky, northern coasts. There, sea otters dine on sea urchins.

blue-footed
boobies

whitetip
reef shark

Whitetip reef sharks hunt in the
Pacific Ocean. On the Galápagos
Islands, blue-footed boobies rest
on shore.

Steller sea lions dive for squid. Blobfish swim deep below the surface. The Pacific Ocean is filled with many special creatures!

blobfish

Steller sea lions

Fast Facts About the Pacific Ocean

Size: 60.1 million square miles (155.6 million square kilometers); largest ocean

Average Depth: 12,795 feet (3,900 meters)

Greatest Depth: 36,201 feet (11,034 meters)

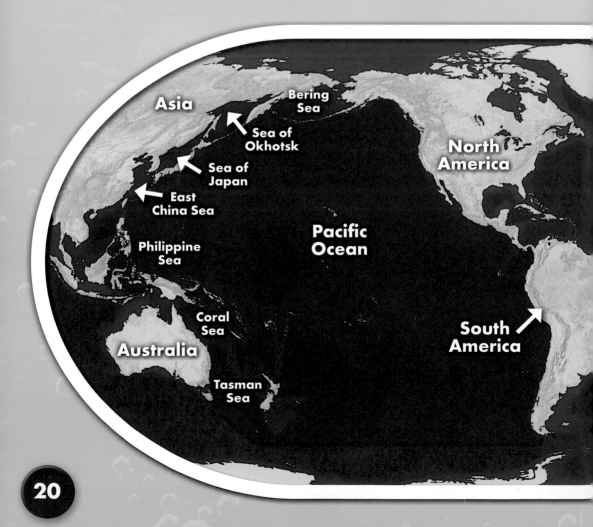

Asia

Bering Sea

Sea of Okhotsk

Sea of Japan

East China Sea

North America

Philippine Sea

Pacific Ocean

Coral Sea

Australia

South America

Tasman Sea

Major Bodies of Water: Sea of Okhotsk, Bering Sea, Sea of Japan, East China Sea, Philippine Sea, Coral Sea, Tasman Sea

Continents Touched: Asia, Australia, South America, North America

Total Coastline: 84,297 miles (135,663 kilometers)

Top Natural Resources: oil, natural gas, tuna, salt, gravel

Famous Shipwrecks:
- *Two Brothers* (1823)
- *Amaranth* (1913)
- *USS Arizona* (1941)
- *Asama Maru* (1944)

USS Arizona

Glossary

climate—the weather patterns in an area over a long period of time

coral reef—a structure made of coral that usually grows in shallow seawater

currents—large patterns of water movement in an ocean

earthquakes—disasters in which the ground shakes because of the movement of rock deep underground

El Niño—a series of weather patterns in the Pacific Ocean that affect weather around the world

equator—an imaginary line around the center of Earth; the equator divides the planet into a northern half and a southern half.

hemispheres—halves of the globe; the equator and the International Date Line divide Earth into different hemispheres.

kelp—a large seaweed

phytoplankton—tiny ocean plants that drift

plates—huge, moving pieces of Earth's surface

trenches—deep and narrow cuts in the ocean floor

tropical—part of the tropics; the tropics is a hot, rainy region near the equator.

typhoons—tropical storms with strong winds and rain

volcanoes—holes in the earth; when a volcano erupts, hot, melted rock called lava shoots out.

To Learn More

AT THE LIBRARY

Chin, Jason. *Island: A Story of the Galápagos.* New York, N.Y.: Roaring Brook Press, 2012.

Schuetz, Kari. *Life in a Coral Reef.* Minneapolis, Minn.: Bellwether Media, 2016.

Spilsbury, Louise and Richard. *Pacific Ocean.* Chicago, Ill.: Capstone Heinemann Library, 2015.

ON THE WEB

Learning more about the Pacific Ocean is as easy as 1, 2, 3.

1. Go to www.factsurfer.com.

2. Enter "Pacific Ocean" into the search box.

3. Click the "Surf" button and you will see a list of related web sites.

With factsurfer.com, finding more information is just a click away.

Index

animals, 5, 10, 11, 16, 17, 18, 19

Atlantic Ocean, 4

climate, 8, 9, 16

continents, 6, 7, 10, 11

coral reef, 11

currents, 10

earthquakes, 15

El Niño, 9

equator, 6, 8

floor, 5

Galápagos Islands, 10, 18

Great Barrier Reef, 11

hemispheres, 6

location, 6, 7

Magellan, Ferdinand, 5

maps, 6, 7, 13, 20, 21

Mariana Trench, 5

mountains, 13

name, 5

plants, 5, 16, 17

plates, 15

Ring of Fire, 12, 13, 15

seas, 6

size, 4, 5

surface, 5, 16, 19

trenches, 5, 13, 15

typhoons, 9

volcanoes, 12, 13

The images in this book are reproduced through the courtesy of: Lee Yiu Tung, front cover (left); Matt9122, front cover (right); Mark Schwettmann, p. 4; Jason Isley -Scubazoo/ Science Faction/ Corbis, p. 5; kwest, p. 8; Marvin Dembinsky Photo Associates/ Alamy, p. 9 (top); China Stringer Network/ Reuters/ Newscom, p. 9 (bottom); Jess Kraft, p. 10; Debra James, p. 11; Nature Picture Library/ Alamy, p. 12; Justin Gilligan/ OceanwideImages.com, p. 14; Ethan Daniels, pp. 16-17; Aleksey Stemmer, p. 17 (top); worldswildlifewonders, p. 17 (center); Joe Belanger, p. 17 (bottom); Holger Mette, p. 18 (top); Yann hubert, p. 18 (bottom); Kerryn Parkinson/ Norfanz/ Zuma Press, p. 19 (top); Kenneth Canning, p. 19 (bottom); Douglas Peebles/ Corbis, p. 21.